JUN 1 1 2004

DINOSAUR HUNTERS

DINOSAUR HUNTERS

Uncovering the Hidden Remains of Canada's Ancient Giants

HISTORY/BIOGRAPHY

by Lisa Murphy-Lamb

PUBLISHED BY ALTITUDE PUBLISHING CANADA LTD.
1500 Railway Avenue, Canmore, Alberta T1W 1P6
www.altitudepublishing.com
1-800-957-6888

Extreme care has been taken to ensure that all information presented in
this book is accurate and up to date. Neither the author nor the
publisher can be held responsible for any errors.

Publisher	Stephen Hutchings
Associate Publisher	Kara Turner
Editors	Colleen Anderson, Kara Turner, Jill Foran

We acknowledge the financial support of the Government
of Canada through the Book Publishing Industry Development
Program (BPIDP) for our publishing activities.

Altitude GreenTree Program
Altitude Publishing will plant twice as many trees as were used
in the manufacturing of this product.

National Library of Canada Cataloguing in Publication Data
Murphy-Lamb, Lisa
    Dinosaur hunters : uncovering the hidden remains of Canda's ancient
    giants / Lisa Murphy-Lamb

    (Amazing stories)
    Includes bibliographical references
    ISBN 1-55153-982-9

    1. Paleontology--Canada, Western--History--Anecdotes. 2.
    Paleontologists--Canada--Biography. I. Title. II. Series: Amazing
    stories (Canmore, Alta.)
    QE707.A2M87 2003   560'.922712   C2003-910899-6

Printed and bound in Canada by Friesens
2 4 6 8 9 7 5 3 1

The front cover shows the bones of a *Tyrannosaurus rex* on view
at the Royal Tyrrell Museum (Photograph by Barry Jennings, ViewCalgary)

Note: This book is not intended to be read as a scientific study. Stories and facts have been
taken from historical records, biographies, and photos. Fictionalized details were then added
to the facts to create stories around the amazing lives of seven fascinating dinosaur hunters.

To Maxwell and Charlie, because
dinosaurs still roam freely in their world,
and to James, with love, for encouraging me to write.

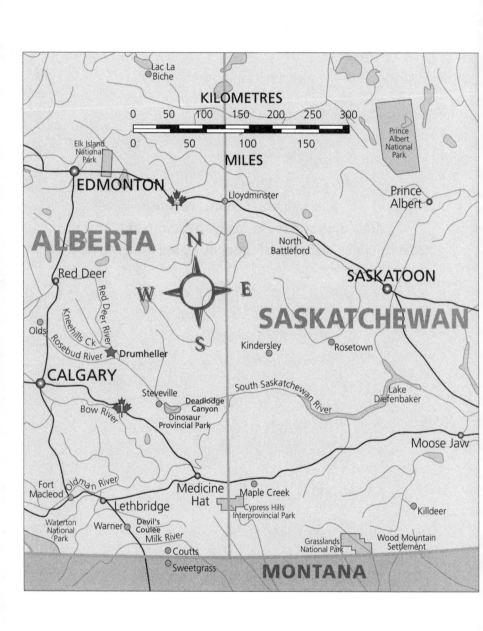

Contents

Prologue 11

Chapter 1 Canada's First Dinosaur
    Hunter: George Dawson 13

Chapter 2 Dinosaur Bones and Coal:
    Joseph B. Tyrrell 27

Chapter 3 A Family of Dinosaur
    Hunters: The Sternbergs 49

Chapter 4 The Great Canadian
    Dinosaur Rush 64

Chapter 5 War and Change 84

Chapter 6 A Modern Dinosaur Hunter:
    Philip Currie 94

Epilogue 113

Bibliography 114

Appendix 1: Dinosaur Data 117

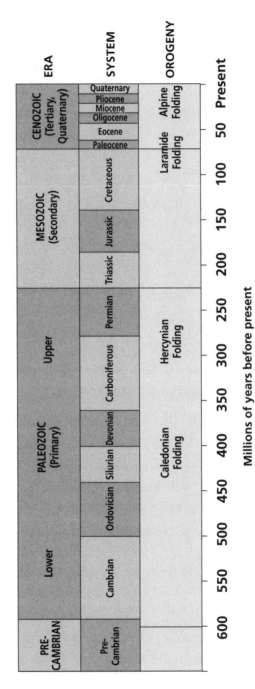

The Geological Time Scale

Prologue

He walks along the footpath of the familiar land, the dry earth crunching beneath his boots, a small chisel swinging from his belt. The air is hot and dusty, and the retreating sun casts a warm, orange glow on the canyon walls. He likes to climb alone at this time of day, when his responsibilities with the fossil hunting party are over and he can explore the maze of wind-carved hoodoos in peace.

The rock outcroppings running along the steep cliff sides tell the stories of ancient history: a grey rock layer indicates a time when forests covered the land; a sandy layer is all that is left behind by the fast-flowing rivers that once flooded the area. The dinosaur bones are sealed in the sandstone layer. This is what he's here for.

The sun is sinking low and the mosquitoes are out in force. He should turn back. It will be dark soon and he does not want to get lost in the labyrinth of pinnacles and hoodoos. But what if the next turn he makes brings him to a bone or an overlooked bed of dinosaur remains? He knows that as each season progresses, more dinosaur bones are revealed by the elements at work on the canyon walls.

At the end of the ridge he sees nothing but loose rock and another deep gully ahead. Noting the sun's crouched position, he knows he must head back to camp. But as he turns to go, he suddenly slips and loses his balance. His misstep upsets the dirt at his feet and reveals what he is looking for.

He stoops, pokes a long forefinger into the dust, and uncovers what looks like a piece of rock. But it is not just a rock. It is a fossilized bone with a dense outer layer — the bone of a carnivore. His heart pounds and he quickly forgets about his tired and aching muscles. He feels only the hard surface of the dinosaur bone and the incredible rush of discovery. Where there is one bone, there are likely to be others.

Chapter 1
Canada's First Dinosaur Hunter: George Dawson

George Dawson jumped down from the creaking wooden seat at the front of the wagon, relieved to have survived the last leg of his journey from Montreal. With the driver's liquor breath still lingering in his nostrils, George was trying hard to put the treacherous trip out of his mind. His tension began to ease as he focussed on the stunning prairie landscape that surrounded him.

It was the summer of 1874, and George was thrilled to be back on western soil. Hired as a geologist and naturalist by the Canadian Boundary Commission the year before, he was one of 270 men tasked with marking the border between Canada and the United States. Astronomers, surveyors, topographers, engineers, surgeons, veterinarians, photographers, cooks, tailors, carpenters, wheelwrights, bakers, and blacksmiths had all begun the job of marking the border a year and a half earlier. George had joined the group, already a year into the project, at Lake of the Woods. By the end of two summers, he had walked 1280 kilometres of border, leaving behind 388 posts and earthen mounds to mark the frontier.

Now, after spending a long, cold winter in Montreal, George was eager to get back to work. He and his colleagues reunited in the frontier town of Fort Dufferin, Manitoba, and though the weather was hot and the mosquitoes were swarming, George went to sleep that night feeling excited about the adventures that lay ahead.

The next morning, George rose before sun-up and joined the others for breakfast around the fire. The tents, still frozen from the frosty night air, would be dismantled before they set off to complete the day's tasks. The crisp, early morning air filled George's lungs and confirmed for him once again that his decision to travel west had been a wise one.

George Dawson was a young man, 24 years old and recently out of school. He had studied at McGill College and then overseas at the London Royal School of Mines. His mother had suggested a career as a professor, and though he loved his mother dearly and would do almost anything to please her, his father had helped him to set his sights on an entirely different career.

As a child, George had spent many happy days exploring the semi-wooded campus of McGill College, where his father, paleobotanist Sir William Dawson, served as principal. Then one day, when George was just nine years old, he was diagnosed with an illness that would greatly affect his carefree boyhood. This illness was a rare form of tuberculosis called Potts disease. A painful affliction, it softened and collapsed the vertebrae in George's spine, forcing the young boy to wear a body truss and spend most of seven years in bed.

Though the bed-ridden George could no longer explore the great outdoors, his father would often bring the great outdoors to him. Usually, bags of scientific specimens and piles of beautifully illustrated nature books surrounded George's sickbed. Tutors were also hired to help George keep up with his studies. A bright boy with a desire to learn, George read the classics: the novels of Dickens, the poems of Tennyson and Byron, and his father's own geological textbook. George eagerly examined the fossils, insects, and plants that his father brought to him, and devoured every word of his father's stories. He dreamed of the world beyond his bedroom and vowed he would return to explore it.

When the headaches and relentless back pain finally stopped, George was ready to live his life again; and he was ready to live it outdoors. Of course, it wouldn't be easy. The disease had curved his shoulders and stunted his growth, leaving the young man with a hunched back and the stature of a 11-year-old boy.

After completing his post-secondary studies, George, under guidance from his father, accepted a position with the Canadian Border Commission. However, when he met the rest of the survey team, he immediately saw their sceptical looks and heard their mocking tones. The men didn't take him seriously. George quickly let them know he would not tolerate their sneers, nor would he accept their pity.

Day after day, the survey team traced the 49th parallel through mud and swampland, across raging rivers, and over thigh-high grass. George walked or rode his horse for hours, his head down, his eyes and

George Dawson, third from the right on the back row, photographed
with his colleagues from the Canadian Boundary Commission

mind alert. He looked a sight riding a horse. Small in
stature, he barely sat higher than the horse's head,
and he rode hunched over, as if he had been studying
books late into the night. Face serious and intent,
legs gripping the sides of the animal, George would
ignore the complaints of his fellow workers and forge
ahead along a route, regardless of the obstacles that
lay in his path.

While he kept busy marking the border, George

also undertook scientific studies of his surroundings along the way. Each day by dusk, his collection bag would be bulging, heavy with additions to his cherished collection from the natural world. George worked hard to prove himself as a valuable geologist worthy of such outdoor pursuits. He diligently photographed and recorded every detail of the specimens he amassed each day.

It took a while, but the other men on George's team finally began to look beyond his physical characteristics. He had proven himself to be tough; indeed, tougher than most. Before long, his dogged determination and confidence had inspired a score of men to work harder.

At night, after his specimens were organized and his notes updated, George would sit down by the campfire, roll his first of many cigarettes, and let his seriousness fade away. Once the sun had gone down, he let the other men see his softer side, regaling them with stories and even cracking the odd joke. He also liked to listen to his colleagues tell stories about their lives and families back home. George had had no time to find a wife or start a family of his own. Science was his first love, and it was all-consuming.

Adventures En Route

George sat inside his tent and recorded the day's events in his journal. It was a hot summer's evening. The tension in his shoulders and back from the day's work subsided as he organized his notes. Through his canvas wall he could hear the beating of Native drums in the distance. Half-starved dogs circled his tent looking for food. He banged on the soft wall to scare them off before returning to his diary.

As George continued to write, a rustling sound outside began to distract him. Annoyed, he stuck his head out of the tent, ready to throw a pebble at a returning dog. But there was no dog to be seen. Instead, he caught a fleeting glimpse of a dark, mysterious figure as it disappeared from his line of sight. Curious, George put his journal aside, and left his tent to investigate.

He followed voices to the campfire. Standing back in the night shadows, his rifle at his side, George surveyed the scene. Two Native men had come to talk with the survey party. Intrigued, George listened.

The visitors had brought a translator.

"What have you come for?" the translator asked.

The surveyors explained that they were there to map the land and look for mineral resources.

Seeking more information, the translator

inquired, "On whose authority are you here? Where do you go next?"

George heard the men in his party explain that they were there on behalf of the Canadian government to mark the exact separation between Canada and the United States, and to map the land along the Canadian side of the border. Assurances were made to the Native men that the party meant no harm and would soon be moving on. After listening to their explanation, the Peigan men told the representatives of the Boundary Commission to let their superiors know that they did not wish to have their land surveyed. It was native land. The country north of the border belonged to them, not to the government of Canada.

The survey party had been warned about the dangers of the West; it was rumoured that Native peoples, whisky runners, and outlaws liked to make life hard for surveyors. But George did not fear the Native peoples. He was intrigued by the traditional Native stories he heard along the route, some of which offered spiritual explanations for the very phenomena he was trying to elucidate scientifically.

As George lay in bed pondering the day's events, the smoky smell of burning smudge was replaced by something stronger. Suddenly, there was commotion in the camp. George scrambled out of his tent to see a prairie fire raging on both sides of the creek, not far from where the tents were pitched. Urged on by strong winds, the fire gained momentum. Ashes and plumes of smoke filled the men's lungs. Tying water-soaked oat sacks on the ends of sticks, the men beat the burning earth in hopes of obstructing the fire's path. They worked well into the night to save their camp. Exhausted and overwhelmed by the fire's power, they eventually sought refuge in the creek and let the flames pass, saving what they could of their camp.

Wheezing and covered in soot, George watched the fire burn in the distance. What a land he worked on. A land characterized by the unexpected, both pleasant and dangerous.

The group continued on their way across the scorched prairies. After several hours of walking, George looked up from the burnt plains and stretched. He had been travelling with his head down and his eyes focussed on the ground for most of the day. His collection bag bulged. As he stretched his sore muscles, George noticed that storm clouds had formed and the sky had darkened. After countless days of dry, blistering heat, it was finally about to rain. Judging from the heaviness in his step, George knew it was time to take a real break and join the men who had already assembled for lunch. Within minutes, the rain began to fall.

Taking shelter from the downpour, George sat under a Red River cart and attempted to eat what the cook had prepared. He was hungry, for he had already walked more than seven hours that day. But his bread was soggy and his plate of food was half full of water. Setting down his sodden lunch, George pulled his hat over his eyes and waited patiently for the downpour to end.

Once the rain stopped, surveying tasks were resumed. George returned to his exploration of the area's geology. Checking his map, he located the team's position just west of the village of Killdeer and south of the Wood Mountain settlement. He then retraced his steps to a coulee that had caught his attention before lunch. Prodding his bony finger into the ancient sediments of the coulee, George pried loose small chunks of earth to take a closer look. There, poking out of the earth, was what looked like a fragment of fossilized bone. The part sticking out of the bank had been washed clean in the recent rains.

For a moment, George was unable to touch the fossil. He was immobilized by myriad thoughts rushing through his mind. If this was a bone, what type of animal was it from? After a few seconds, he relaxed and bent down to investigate.

It was indeed a bone, which over millions of years had turned into a fossil — a piece of history immortalized in stone. George took his geologist's hammer firmly in his hand and began excavating the rock and earth around the bone. At that moment, nothing else mattered. He was so focussed on his task that everything but the bone ceased to exist.

Finally the fragment of bone was freed from the earth. George brushed off the loose dirt and examined his find. Over time, minerals in the surrounding rock and soil had leached into the bone and turned it a shade of dark yellow. It was also cracked in places, but it was still clearly recognizable as a piece of bone. George stood for a moment, trembling, trying not to shout out in excitement at his discovery. The others already regarded him as an odd little man, and hollering to the heavens would not do much to improve his reputation. But he was euphoric. He knew that what he held in his hands was an important find, even if he was unsure of exactly what it was.

George bent down and continued to dig. Forgetting about the other workers, he methodically cleared away the overburden. His hunch proved correct. Beneath the dirt lay more bones. Adjusting the angle of his hammer, he let the shape of each fossil guide his incisions. When the next bone came loose, George was surprised at its size. The fossilized bones were larger than any he had ever seen.

George worked feverishly all day, fuelled by his desire to understand exactly what it was that he had discovered. He dug until he was satisfied that he had unearthed as much as he could from the bone bed. He was still not certain what kind of animal the bones belonged to, but he had a hunch.

During his studies at McGill and at the London School of Mines, George had read scientific papers about the fossilized remains of what were then believed to be giant lizards. Sir Richard Owen, a surgeon, bone collector, and Britain's leading anatomist, had coined the term "Dinosauria," meaning terrible lizard. George believed that he, too, had found fossilized dinosaur bones, but it was some time before he knew with certainty what he had discovered.

Knowing that no one in Canada was qualified to scientifically identify the bones he had unearthed, George had them sent to Philadelphia, Pennsylvania, to be identified by Dr. Edward Cope. Dr. Cope was a leading American paleontologist, and one of the great American bone hunters. When George finally received word from Cope, he learned that the bones were hadrosaurian, that of a duckbill dinosaur. George also received recognition for being the first scientist to discover dinosaur bones in Canada.

* * *

George Dawson left the Boundary Commission after two years of service, and joined the Geological Survey of Canada as a head geologist with a remit to explore British Columbia and determine if the land had agricultural and mineral resource potential. By 1877, he was leading his own group of men to map the coalfields of Alberta.

George spent most of his career with the Geological Survey, making significant contributions to the scientific knowledge of the West. He explored, photographed, and documented the Haida way of life in the Queen Charlotte Islands. He trekked across the prairies, through northern British Columbia, and up to the Yukon. He made it as far north as the Bering Sea, where he was hired to help settle a fishing dispute between the U.S. and foreign fishing boats.

In the Yukon, George used his scientific knowledge to locate minerals other than coal. His maps of the Yukon were in great demand during the Gold Rush, and his meticulous reports of where to find gold made many a miner a rich man.

Dawson City is named after George, as is a bay in Manitoba, a mountain and glacier in British Columbia, and the Dawson Range of mountains in the Yukon. Every map of Canada bears his name and remembers his contributions.

In 1874, George Dawson became the first Canadian to find and record dinosaur bones in western Canada. It would be another 10 years before the next recorded dinosaur bones would be discovered.

Chapter 2

Dinosaur Bones and Coal: Joseph B. Tyrrell

hen he was a child, Joseph Tyrrell spent most of his free time scrambling along the banks of the Humber River or roaming the open fields and forests surrounding his family's Weston, Ontario home. His bedroom was a miniature zoo, harbouring every spider and grasshopper he managed to collect. Live specimens could also be found in other parts of his parents' house; the bathtub often served as a temporary home for his pet crayfish and mud turtles.

Joseph loved everything about the outdoors.

Unfortunately, tragedy struck the young boy when an attack of scarlet fever kept him confined to his bed for quite some time. When he was able to return to the fields and forests, he needed glasses to see and an ear trumpet to hear. Even so, his love for adventure was as strong as ever. As time passed, Joseph's passion for exploring the outdoors continued to grow. He vowed to make exploration his life's work.

Raised by a strict and pious mother and a well-to-do stonemason father, Joseph was taught to be a dutiful son. His dreams of exploration were largely put aside while he studied law at the University of Toronto, fulfilling his father's wishes. But during this time, Joseph didn't completely bury his passion for the natural sciences. Whenever he could, he stole away from the stuffy law library and devoured books on the plant and animal kingdoms.

Then pneumonia hit. It weakened his body but strengthened his resolve to return to the outdoors. With his doctor as an ally, Joseph convinced his parents that his health was an important reason to work and live outdoors. Suddenly freed from his filial duties, Joseph pursued a position with the Geological Survey of Canada.

His first job with the Survey as a third-class clerk was no more physically demanding than that of a lawyer. He worked in a basement office identifying, describing, and labelling collections of rocks and fossils. But while this job was not exactly what he had envisioned for himself, it gave him a quick education in geology and a foot in the door to work as a surveyor.

Soon enough, Joseph's intelligence and strength of character were noticed, and within a year and a half of being hired by the Survey, he began his career as an explorer in the Canadian West. He was sent off to help geologist George Dawson chart the unknown country of the West, collect biological samples, and locate coal and other minerals.

A New Life
The year was 1883. Under the great arching prairie sky, 25-year-old Joseph Tyrrell pounded the final tent peg into the bone-dry earth. New to this way of life, he was very eager and alert. Not so long ago he had been praticing law in Ottawa. But his life as a lawyer, as well his family's 24-room mansion and the hearty home-cooked meals he had always enjoyed, were now a part of his past. He had travelled a long way to join George Dawson and his team of surveyors in Winnipeg. And he was ready to work.

Joseph stepped back and looked at the canvas walls of his new home. The tent would hardly keep

Joseph Tyrrell as a young man

him safe from the dangers outside; dangers he had heard about over and over through the many folk stories his grandmother had told him when he was a child. Stories of the West had been filled with descriptions of disease, wild animal attacks, mosquitoes large enough to hitch and plough with, and hostile

Native peoples. The tales were still so vivid in his memory that Joseph had stiffened and reached for his revolver the first time he had heard the distant cries of coyotes and the unfamiliar sounds of diving nighthawks. But despite his initial fear, he knew that his grandmother's stories were, for the most part, nothing more than tall tales.

Joseph loved a good story, but more importantly, he loved discovering the facts behind that story. Stories were for calming tired boys and for building dreams upon. But stories alone did not sustain the curious mind of a man. Joseph did not leave Ontario in search of stories. He left because of them.

Joseph revelled in the glorious sights, smells, and sounds surrounding the camp. He loved the endless prairies, and the way their native grasses rippled in the wind. At that time, there were no roads. Travel through the thick grasses and muddy muskeg would be on foot, on horseback, or by buckboard. What would his parents think of his new life?

The Lawless West
Joseph experienced frontier life first-hand while working with George Dawson in the West. In Fort Macleod, where the Geological Survey purchased new supplies, there was a North West Mounted Police

base. There, Joseph met the brave men who had been sent west to establish law and order. The North West Mounted Police issued strong warnings to Joseph and Dawson about the Native bandits, horse thieves, and whisky traders who operated throughout the West. But Joseph was only half-listening as he remembered a story he once heard. It was about a wind that blew so strong and steady in Fort Macleod that it lifted a cow high up against a barn. The cow was held there for so long that it starved to death before it was returned to the ground below.

George Dawson more or less ignored the police warnings, and he and his men left Fort Macleod determined to get on with their work. But Dawson did take some precautions. He purchased extra guns and ammunition, and ordered members of his party to take turns as outriders, riding ahead into coulees and hiding spots and searching out possible ambushes.

Every night, a guard was posted in the camp. Whenever it was his turn to act as guard, Joseph stayed awake by recalling his grandmother's wild stories. He wasn't worried about his own safety because he was a good shot. He had learned how to handle a gun early on in his life, and could put out a candle flame at 20 paces. Once, he had even shot 12 rabbits with 12 shots.

Dinosaur Bones and Coal: Joseph B. Tyrrell

Always on the lookout for potential danger, Joseph and the rest of the party made their way along the banks of the Oldman River, heading upstream into the foothills of the Rocky Mountains. At the Crowsnest Pass, the expedition officially began.

On the first morning of the expedition, as the sun began to edge over the mountains, the men warmed themselves by the fire with a strong cup of tea, then breakfasted on fried bacon and bread. After breakfast, Dawson assigned Joseph his first job as a surveyor; a job that would see him through the rest of the summer.

Joseph quickly learned his task. There were no topographical maps of Canada in the 1880s, and so the party had to create maps as they went. Joseph's job was to measure distance in paces. With a compass in one hand and a canvas collection bag on his side, he embarked on daily, evenly paced walks. He had to record every 100 set of paces that he walked. To keep track, he placed a new stick in his pocket after every set of 100 steps. At the end of several hours, he counted the number of sticks in his trousers, wrote down how many sets of 100 he had walked, and started again.

As he worked, Joseph tried to ignore the scorching heat and windless air. He also tried to ignore the mosquitoes that pestered him and bit his fingers until they swelled to the size of sausages. Of course, it wasn't just mosquitoes that he encountered; deer, elk, and bears often crossed his path.

Once while he was working, Joseph kicked a bush in which a bear slept. Disturbed from its nap, the growling bear ambled off down the riverbank. Another time, a grizzly chose to use the same narrow mountain path that Joseph was using. The two came face to face, and the grizzly rose onto its hind legs and growled at Joseph. Wanting at all costs to avoid both an attack by the bear and a fatal tumble down the rocky cliff, Joseph raised his rifle and killed the grizzly, sending it tumbling down the mountainside. Then he continued climbing.

Many men on the expedition thought that pace surveying was repetitive and monotonous, but Joseph was doing what he loved. Unfazed by the solitude, the wildlife, and the intolerable heat, he walked an even pace each and every day. Joseph's love of the land and his poor eyesight had taught him to examine things closely. It was this tendency for close examination that led him to his first major discovery.

While out on a typical daily trek, Joseph, head down and eyes alert, spotted a protruding outcrop on the rough ground. He began to chip at the rocky area, first with his boot and then with his geologist's hammer. Several chips at the black rock confirmed that it was a coal seam about the size of his leg. Coal was the major purpose of George Dawson's expedition. His pulse quickening, Joseph chipped off a sample of his discovery and retraced his steps.

As he walked towards the camp, Joseph had difficulty keeping his mind on his pace counting. He knew that he had made an important discovery and was anxious to show the coal sample to Dawson. The coal seam that Joseph discovered that day would eventually provide the economic basis for the town of Fernie, British Columbia.

Upon his discovery, Joseph became a respected geologist. He finished his summer with Dawson's team at Kicking Horse Pass, then caught a ride to Calgary on a construction train. He then returned to Ottawa, fully possessed by life in the Canadian West.

Exploring the Badlands
After spending a grey winter in Ottawa, the 26-year-old Joseph headed west once again. This time, he returned as a head surveyor for the Geological Survey of Canada.

The value of his coal find the year before was considered tremendous. Backed solidly by George

Dawson and Prime Minister Sir John A. MacDonald (who was a friend of Joseph's father), Joseph had been rewarded for this find with his own team and his own land to explore. This land consisted of an 18,210-hectare area in Alberta.

Joseph was given a project that covered the geological district north of Calgary and east of the Rockies, from the Bow River to the Saskatchewan River. Early French trappers and traders had named this area *Les mauvaises terres*, or badlands, a name that made reference to an inhospitable landscape characterized by eroded and steeply sloped channels and gullies.

Although the surveying project would span three years, Joseph proved his worth within the first two months of leaving Ottawa. Using Calgary as his base, he bought a canoe, a buckboard, five horses, tents, blankets, and a supply of food. He hired a team of three assistants — two Native men and an American — to drive the horses, do the cooking and chores, and pitch the tents.

At the edge of the Red Deer River Valley, Joseph's party followed Rosebud Creek and Kneehills Creek and set up camp on the valley floor. It was an idyllic spot: flat, with an abundance of wood, water, and grass. There was plenty to examine in the rocks and, wasting no time, Joseph plunged into the uncharted badlands to survey the mineral deposits, collect fossils, and determine elevations.

The canyon sides of the badlands were characterized by sheer red walls that were dissected by deep runnels. Evident in the cliffs were alternating layers of grey sandstone, reddish siltstone, black coal, and fragments of volcanic rock. These rock layers told the stories of ancient deltas, lakes, forests, and tropical swamps that once covered the land.

On a particularly stifling July day in 1884, a peculiar brown object in a canyon wall caught his eye. Curious, he climbed up the steep slope and brushed some dirt away from the wall. The outline of a fossil appeared. On closer inspection, Joseph could make out the distinct shape of a jawbone. He took out his hammer and cleared away the loose rock and dirt until he was able to extract the jawbone carefully. Slowly turning it over, he examined it from every angle. Unsure what species of animal it belonged to, he laid it on the ground and carefully mapped its location.

With that job done, Joseph focussed his attention back to the slope. He noticed there were other fossil bones littered along the canyon walls below him. Carefully, he made his way down to a ledge strewn with bones and other fossils. There he found a vertebra, and then a tooth. The tooth was large and had serrated edges. Clearly it had belonged to a carnivore, but what kind of carnivore?

Once again, Joseph thought of a Native legend his grandmother had told him. This time the tale was about large water monsters that had roamed the earth long before man. These monsters were covered with red hair, and they sported horns in the middle of their foreheads. According to the legend, the monsters also fought with giant thunderbirds, and those that died in battle turned to stone. Over the years the monsters' petrified bones had mixed with the remains of seashells and turtles and were scattered throughout the badlands.

Joseph wondered if the tooth he held came from such a prehistoric creature. Sitting on a ridge that overlooked his small excavation site, he surveyed his finds, pulled a notebook out of his bag, and wrote a letter to his father. It read:

My dearest Father,
Today I made the most amazing discovery. I'm not sure what it is but it is unlike anything else I have ever seen. The skull is nearly perfectly preserved, but I'm not sure how to categorize it. I can only think it is a creature from a time beyond our fathoming . . .

Dinosaur Bones and Coal: Joseph B. Tyrrell

Joseph lay his notebook down and, feeling the warm dusty breeze on his skin, remembered George Dawson's discovery 10 years earlier. Were these bones like the hadrosaurian bones Dawson had found? Were there more? Joseph kicked thoughtfully at the soft dirt.

Three days later, he was in his canoe. Powered by the swift current of the Red Deer River, Joseph looked for evidence of coal in the layers of ancient rock that formed the shoreline.

The search paid off, for on June 12, 1884, just three days after discovering the large deposit of fossilized dinosaur bones, Joseph fulfilled his obligations to the Geological Survey of Canada. He located one of the greatest coal deposits in all of Canada. It was the coal seam that would support the coal-mining industry for the town of Drumheller. This was good news indeed.

A Startling Discovery

The bone bed and significant coal seam were great discoveries, but Joseph knew there was more to uncover in the badlands. He had a feeling that he had merely scratched the surface of an ancient graveyard rich with mineral deposits.

Later that summer, as Joseph continued to

explore the badlands, he spotted a bull snake sunning itself on a rock ledge. Noting that the slumbering reptile was a descendent of the reptiles that had lived with the dinosaurs, Joseph took the snake as a good omen.

As the sun rose high in the sky and coloured the rocks a bright orange, Joseph left camp to do some exploring. Intrigued by a section of exposed rock on a nearby slope, he clambered up to it. He took a moment to catch his breath, and then something caught his eye.

He leaned in closer for a better look. There, partially covered in the sun-baked earth, was a great skull with rows of sharp teeth grinning up at him.

Startled, Joseph jumped back, caught himself, then dropped to his knees and began to move the loose dirt away. Soon enough he had exposed the rest of the jawbone. It had two rows of serrated teeth that he was certain once tore into the flesh of other animals. The skull was very large, unlike that of any animal still roaming the badlands of Alberta. The prehistoric past literally stared Joseph in the face. But how far into the past was he looking? How many years had this skull been waiting to scare the wits out of him?

Joseph shouted to the others, grabbed his axe

and the small geologist's hammer that lay beside him in the dust, and began to chip away at the rock and earth that surrounded the skull.

He and his group dug well into the day. Along with the skull, they uncovered a complete skeleton cemented in the hardened earth. Thighbones and ribs lay beside the rest of the bones that had once supported the great weight of the skull.

As the dinner hour approached, Joseph stood back, wiped a grimy hand across his brow, and smiled at the newly excavated pile of fossil bones. It had been a good day. There, lying before him, were silent relics of the past. These relics were in the form of broken, brittle bones, but they all had stories to tell. Lifting a cracked and aged tooth, Joseph let his imagination run wild as he pictured the beast's last meal:

The gigantic form of a meat-eating dinosaur crashes through the trees. In its teeth it carries the lifeless body of a small plant-eating dinosaur. The enormous dinosaur charges into a clearing and drops its meal to the ground. Ripping and tearing into its prey with its sharp teeth and fearsome claws, the dinosaur devours the carcass in minutes.

Joseph returned the tooth to the pile and called his men to his side. Their job had only just begun. The bones were too big and heavy to move all at once. The team had only one canoe and a horse and wagon, and it was 60 kilometres to Fort Calgary from their location near Kneehills Creek. They would have to choose only the best bones to take with them, and the rest of the fossils would have to be stockpiled.

The men carefully secured the heavy skull to a buckboard, lifting it onto the back of the wagon using improvised stretchers. They then selected the best of the bones and teeth, and prepared the fossils for the rough journey to Fort Calgary.

The trip progressed slowly as the team cautiously planned the smoothest route to take across the roadless prairies. Despite the careful selection process, the wagon was heavily loaded and the journey was tough on the wheels. The axles broke many times as the wagon struggled over muddy trails and through thick grasses. Joseph and the men fashioned makeshift axles from branches of spruce trees to keep them moving.

One week later, the fossilized bones made it to Fort Calgary. And thanks to the careful planning of Joseph's team, the damage to the bones was minimal. The treasured fossils were then sent east by train to the Geological Survey of Canada headquarters in Ottawa for identification.

Eventually, word got back to Joseph. The skull and bones were initially identified as *Laelaps incrassates*, but were later reclassified as *Albertosaurus sarcophagus*. This flesh-eating dinosaur of Alberta was an early cousin of the massive *Tyrannosaurus rex*, and Joseph was the first to discover the species.

Albertosaurus sarcophagus is one member of a small family of conquering theropods (meat-eaters). These dinosaurs lived in the northern hemisphere during the Cretaceous period, about 65 to 100 million years ago. Smaller than *Tyrannosaurus rex*, *Albertosaurus* walked on two legs and had a large head with sharp, saw-toothed teeth.

After completing his three-year survey of the land south of Edmonton, Joseph was not reassigned to the dinosaur bones in Alberta. As he explored other areas of the Canadian West, he never stopped wondering what other discoveries lay hidden in the earth of the badlands.

A Life of Exploration
Joseph was only 29 when he left Alberta's badlands. He had 70 more years of his adventurous life to live before his name became a memory. He may have

used his father's friendship with then Prime Minister Sir John A. MacDonald to kick-start his profession as an explorer, but it was his intelligence and his knowledge of the land that kept him on the payroll of the Geological Survey.

Joseph's life was never dull, although he did manage to avoid many of the dangers associated with the life of an explorer. He had more use for his geological pick than he ever had for his gun. At times, he did have to hunt to supplement his food supply, and although he never missed a meal, he once wrote that he was sometimes two or three days late for one.

The Native peoples he encountered on his travels, despite looming starvation with the decline of the bison population, were never hostile towards Joseph. However, the surveying teams were often in danger of having their horses stolen while on Native land.

One morning, Joseph woke up to find that all but two of his horses were missing. He offered a Native boy two dollars to find and return the horses, but the boy and the money disappeared as well.

That's when Joseph met Chief Crowfoot. He arranged a meeting and explained his situation, then offered the chief $10 for the return of his horses. Soon enough, the horses were returned and Joseph continued his explorations, a little late but otherwise unharmed.

Joseph Tyrrell eventually married and had three children, although he left his family each summer to conduct more explorations. After surveying the Red Deer River Valley, Joseph led exhibitions in northwest Manitoba. In 1892, he was assigned to explore and survey northern Saskatchewan between the Churchill River and Lake Athabasca. There he learned from the Chippewa guides that there was a river route across the territory known as the Barren Lands, which lead to the coast of the Hudson Bay.

Accompanied by his brother James, Joseph braved rumours of Inuit cannibals, frigid weather, and extreme conditions and trekked across the sub-arctic route not once, but twice. But even with his outstanding contributions to the mapping and exploration of Canada's northwest, Joseph was denied promotion within the Geological Survey. He resigned in December of 1898.

Joseph became a mining consultant in Dawson City at the height of the Gold Rush. His family, how-ever, continued to live in Ottawa, and the times spent apart were difficult. Eventually, the family moved to Toronto, where Joseph worked as a mining consult-ant and a surveyor for the Ontario government.

In 1921, Joseph Tyrrell retired to a country home

Inside the Royal Tyrrell Museum, Drumheller

in the Rouge River valley in Scarborough, Ontario, where he experimented with various strains of apples and transcribed documents tracing the sites of former trading posts. He died in 1957 a wealthy man at the age of 98.

Members of the Geological Survey celebrated Joseph's finds. Because of his discoveries, they began sending trained paleontologists west to hunt specifically for bones. Since the discovery of *Albertosaurus sarcophagus*, hundreds of explorers from all over the world have travelled along the banks of the Red Deer River in search of dinosaur bones.

Joseph Tyrrell sparked the Great Canadian Dinosaur Rush.

* * *

The Royal Tyrrell Museum, a world famous dinosaur museum, was built in Drumheller, Alberta, in 1985. It tells the story of Joseph Tyrrell's early discovery of dinosaur remains in the Red Deer River Valley, and explores what happened in the field of paleontology after that historic event.

Chapter 3
A Family of Dinosaur Hunters: The Sternbergs

With vivid pictures of fierce prehistoric monsters in his head, young Charles Sternberg scrambled over a bale of hay, noisily chasing an older boy. The carnivore-infested swamp of his imagination was really a barn in upper New York State. It was 1860, and 10-year-old Charles was full of energy, harbouring a colourful imagination and a tremendous love of the outdoors.

A ladder leading up to the hayloft seemed the perfect vantage point from which to sight his fleeing friend. Charles climbed effortlessly to the top rung, took a step off, and fell six metres through a hole that had been partially concealed beneath a rug of settling oats. Knocked unconscious, Charles was carried by his older playmate to his mother, who quickly found a doctor.

Charles' head was examined and his leg was bandaged. His imaginary hunting trip had dislocated the fibula and knee of his left leg. From that moment on, his limp would be a reminder of his enthusiastic beginnings as a dinosaur hunter.

Moving West

As a young man, Charles H. Sternberg had heard stories and read theories about the large teeth and bones that were being unearthed in Europe and in the western United States. Benjamin Franklin, a scientist in the 1700s, had believed that God would not allow species of such a large size to become extinct. Franklin believed that these strange creatures still roamed in the unexplored western parts of the country. Charles knew this to be false, but his curiosity had been aroused.

In 1867, Charles finally got the opportunity to see the American West for himself. That year, his father and mother, and eight of his brothers and sisters, packed up the family home in upstate New York and moved west to Kansas. His father was moving in search of employment, but Charles was searching for confirmation of the stories he had heard. He wanted to see for himself the traditions of the Native peoples, the vast bison herds, and the huge expanses of open prairie.

Once settled on the new ranch in Kansas, all the Sternberg children were assigned chores. Charles, who was 17 years old at the time, was responsible for the early morning delivery of produce to a nearby fort. He had to make the delivery by 5 A.M. each morning.

One day while returning from a delivery, pockets full of money from his sales, Charles grew tired. He steered his trusty horse in the direction of home and lay down in the wagon for a nap. He did not wake up for two weeks.

When he arrived home from the market that morning, his brothers found him incoherent. Blood flowed from a single slingshot wound in his forehead. Charles had been attacked and robbed in his sleep. The wound eventually healed, but he lost his hearing in one ear as a result of the attack.

Charles spent as much of each day as he could enjoying the natural world. He wandered the woods and the prairies, where, in the spring, great herds of bison migrated northward. He also followed the news of the men who were making headlines with their fossil finds in the newly opened West.

Spurred by the findings of these men, Charles used whatever spare time he had to hunt for fossils in the chalk beds near his family's ranch. It was here that Charles found his first of many beautiful fossil leaves. This intricate fossilized leaf led him to his life's work.

Charles' father disapproved of his son's fascination with rocks and fossils. He wanted Charles to study something more practical. But Charles was a dreamer, and despite his father's misgivings, he began collecting fossils seriously. At that time, most people did not know that the peculiar rocks with patterns in them were remains of life from millions of years before.

The Life of a Dinosaur Hunter

In 1875, at the age of 25, Charles wrote an earnest letter to eminent paleontologist Edward Drinker Cope, of Philadelphia. In this letter, Charles pleaded with Cope to take him along on a dig. Cope, already committed to a party of hunters, saw promise in the young letter writer and sent him a draft of US$300 to fund his own expedition. His accompanying note said, "I like the style of your letter. Enclosed draft. Go to work."

Armed with proper funds and a consuming desire to uncover the riddles of prehistoric life, Charles acquired a team of ponies, a driver, camp equipment, and tools, and headed to Buffalo Park in Kansas.

The determined young man was committed to a life of fossil hunting. First, though, he needed to prove himself as a dinosaur hunter through patience and hard work. That summer, he searched every corner of Buffalo Park and was rewarded with many fossil finds, all of which he sent east. Later in the season, he was invited to dig with his sponsor, Edward Cope. The two agreed to meet at a train station in Omaha.

Cope, frail, haggard, and swaying in the wind, was waiting on the platform when Charles arrived. Charles, who was wiry, tanned, and stiff-legged from his summer's work, limped towards his new dinosaur-hunting partner. Neither looked like they would be able to endure life in the rugged wilderness, but both had the determination and intensity to do more than just survive. Both men would exceed expectations.

The two dinosaur hunters travelled to Montana, where they soon discovered a scattering of dinosaur bones in a previously unexplored dinosaur graveyard

— so-called for the sheer volume of bones found in a small area. Charles learned competitive bone-hunting techniques from Cope, and was taught how to turn fossils into cash. At the time, Cope was embroiled in a highly publicized feud with another leading paleontologist, Othniel Charles Marsh, the first professor of paleontology at Yale University.

The competitive pair, once friends, were now arch rivals. They had begun their careers at the same time, hiking and hunting for fossils together. But soon they became jealous and suspicious of each other, battling for greater recognition during the so-called "bone wars" of the 1870s and 1880s. It was a period of intense scientific rivalry as the two men fought over territory and raced each other to be the first to make significant new finds.

The feud between Edward Cope and Othniel Marsh inspired a great deal of devious misconduct, and as a result, Charles was sworn to secrecy while working for Cope. Once, he received orders from Cope to go to a location in south central Oregon, where he was to give the local postmaster a secret code. Upon hearing the code, the postmaster would lead him to a field where he was to search for fossils. Charles was not to tell anyone where he was going, nor was he allowed to receive mail while he hunted for bones.

Charles was hard-working and determined, and he soon earned the respect of fellow dinosaur hunters. He was invited on digs throughout the United States, and since he was a freelance hunter, he also worked for Othniel Marsh on occasion. However, Charles remained close friends with Cope, who was originally his mentor, then his boss, and very soon, his peer.

Charles enjoyed many years of successful fossil hunting. It was his chosen career and he managed to make a living at it, albeit sometimes a meagre one. He married and had three sons and a daughter, George (1883), Charles (1885), Maud (1890), and Levi (1894). He encouraged his three sons to join him in the hunt for dinosaurs, and a dynasty was born.

George Sternberg: Accomplished Dinosaur Hunter
Coated in dust, the young George Sternberg enthusiastically held out a large fossil he had just uncovered. It was an excellent specimen of a plesiosaur, a small headed, long necked, marine animal. Both the boy and his father were overjoyed. This find not only made the summer's dig worthwhile, it also served as a sign that nine-year-old George had a talent for digging up dinosaurs.

Even when George was a baby, Charles had

dreamed that his first-born would become a fossil hunter. He had hardly been able to wait to start teaching his son the trade. Each summer, baby George and his mother, Anna, would join Charles on digs, sleeping in a tent, battling howling winds, and enduring the blistering heat. As he got older, George was allowed to tramp behind Charles over the old chalk rocks and look for bones of his own.

At the age of six, George joined his father on a dig. The twosome travelled by horse and buggy over bumpy trails across the American West. Charles was determined to arouse an interest in paleontology in his son. The pair returned with a box full of fossilized leaves and the first of many fossil-hunting stories.

Developing an interest in dinosaurs came as naturally to George as it did to his father. As more years passed, the hunting trips became George's education, and a means of satisfying his ceaseless curiosity about the earth and its history.

By the age of 14, George had quit school to work full-time as his father's apprentice. He learned his father's techniques by working alongside him, excavating fossils from the surrounding rock and earth. George was taught to uncover as much of the bone as he could in order to determine the position in which a skeleton lay. Once confident that he knew the skeleton's position, Charles then taught his son to cut a trench about the width of his hand around the outside of the fossil. This was done so that a frame could be fitted and built around the bones. The exposed parts were then covered with oiled paper and the frame was filled in with plaster. While the plaster dried, George helped his father hammer wood across the frame, creating a lid to what would soon serve as a crate.

Next came the task of digging out the framed crate. It was exhausting work that required either George or his father to lie on one side and chip carefully with a light pick, cutting away just enough stone to loosen the frame. Once the crate and its contents were freed from the earth, more wood would be hammered across the bottom, creating an enclosed crate. This crate would then be packed into a larger crate surrounded by packing material.

During this arduous process, Charles patiently explained to George how this technique had changed over the years. When he first began, Charles used to chip away at each individual bone. He was teaching his son the new technique of removing great slabs of rocks with many bones encased in them. Before long, father and son were able to pass this technique on to the next Sternberg boy, Charlie.

Charlie Sternberg: Reluctant Dinosaur Hunter

Unlike his father and older brother, who knew they were destined to hunt dinosaurs, Charles M. Sternberg, or Charlie, was dragged into the profession.

Charlie was first taken out into the field at the age of seven, when he spent the summer in a tent with his mother and sister while his father and George hunted for fossils. When Charlie was finally old enough to help out, he was already convinced that the work was too hard and the pay too little. Months of cooking meals over smouldering buffalo chips, lugging fossils to horse-drawn wagons, and forging across engorged rivers had confirmed this impression. The life of a dinosaur hunter was difficult, unrewarding, and definitely not for him. Charlie dreamed of being a teacher, or a writer like his grandfather.

So, Charlie stayed at home with his mother and sister while George and his father hunted for bones. He finished high school, and didn't go on his first official collecting expedition until he was 20 years old. He started as head cook, and was responsible for keeping the larder stocked. More than once, though, the food supply ran out in the middle of an intense excavation, and the Sternberg men survived for many days on nothing but potatoes and berries.

Charles Sternberg had even been known to eat the horses' corn in times of desperate need.

After several years of being coerced back out to the field each season to help his father, Charlie chanced upon some remains that finally changed his mind about dinosaur hunting. In 1908, in a rock-walled gorge 150 metres deep, Charlie found the almost complete skeleton of a duckbilled dinosaur, an *Edmontosaurus regalis*. Fossilized along with the bones were a complete skin impression and some of the dinosaur's stomach contents.

Luckily, a fellow American dinosaur hunter who shared the campfire with the Sternbergs that night did not detect Charlie's enthusiasm for his day's find. As Charlie listened to the American hunter boast about his own latest find, also an impression of dinosaur skin, his smile grew wider, but he strove to keep the magnitude of his find to himself. When the hunter complained that is was impossible to collect fossilized skin impressions, Charlie agreed.

Restless with anticipation, Charlie was finally able to get his family alone the next morning. He laughed as he told them of his discovery. Although he had pretended to agree with the hunter the night before, Charlie knew he could excavate the complete dinosaur, skin impressions and all.

Charlie was finally bitten by the dinosaur hunting bug. He knew his younger brother Levi would soon realize his destiny as well.

Levi Sternberg: The Youngest Member of "The Dream Team"

Levi Sternberg was known for his good humour, his pranks, and his hard work. Like his brothers before him, he was introduced to the life of dinosaur hunting at a young age. As soon as he was able to walk, Levi watched his father and older brothers clean their fossils, and he listened to them talk.

As a child, Levi had developed a deep curiosity about dinosaurs. He wanted to hunt with his father and brothers, and hoped he would find a really big dinosaur of his own someday. Because dinosaur hunting had been part of his life since birth, Levi had no delusions about his future. He joined his father and brothers on a full-time basis at the age of 14. By then, Charlie was 23, and George was married with a child on the way.

Life on a dig was tough. It consisted of pitching a tent wherever the group stopped for the night, and eating not much more than beans and wild berries for days on end. Workdays were long and the rewards few and far between. But the thrill of finding a bone more than compensated for the hard work. For years to come, Charles, George, Charlie, and Levi joined forces to hunt for dinosaur bones. They would be referred to as the *Dream Team,* and together they weathered some extreme conditions. Their collective fuel was the discovery of new bones.

Like his brothers, Levi moved up the ranks from student to assistant, and was eventually recognized as an equal to his father within the scientific community.

Tragedy Strikes
The year 1911 brought both tragedy and new opportunity to the Sternbergs. George, by then a father of two, lost his one-year-old daughter when she ate rat poison while playing in the kitchen cupboards. Charles lost his daughter as well. Maud Sternberg, sister to George, Charlie, and Levi, was 20 years old when she died of a mysterious illness.

The Sternbergs worked through their sorrow. George and Charlie busied themselves preparing fossils, Levi continued his studies in high school, and Charles took some time to write about his adventures in the field.

One late winter afternoon, Charlie was preparing a skull of a *Triceratops,* a three-horned ceratopsian with a characteristic neck frill. As he worked, heavy storm clouds formed overhead. Soon, the clouds spun into a funnel-shaped tornado which struck within minutes and shattered the shop where Charlie had been working. Having seen the tornado heading his way, Charlie had escaped moments earlier, but the shop's brick wall had fallen and crushed the *Triceratops* skull. The skull had been intended for the Victoria Memorial Museum in Ottawa (now named the Canadian Museum of Nature), but it was beyond repair.

New Horizons

All the fossils the Sternbergs excavated over the years were sent to museums in London, Paris, and across the United States. But their latest finds, a *Titanotherium* skeleton and a 6-metre long *Platecarpus*, were both promised to Ottawa. *Titanotherium*, more recently referred to as *Brontops*, is an odd-toed ungulate related to modern day horses, tapirs, and rhinoceroses. The *Platecarpus* is a genus of giant marine lizard and is in the family of mosasaurs.

Charles and George were asked by the Ottawa museum to mount the two skeletons. Mounting was a new process to the two oldest Sternbergs, so first they needed to learn the techniques. Father and son decided it was time to see for themselves how their excavated finds were prepared and mounted in the many museums across the U.S.

They boarded a train and visited Pittsburgh, Washington D.C., and New York City, taking every opportunity to observe, ask questions, and study the techniques used to prepare a freestanding mount. Finally, Charles and George arrived in Ottawa, where, after suffering several setbacks, they successfully mounted their *Titanotherium* and *Platecarpus* specimens.

While in Ottawa, Charles signed a contract with the Geological Survey of Canada as head preparator of vertebrate fossils. His sons would be his assistants. Together they would hunt dinosaurs in the province of Alberta. And this time, all their finds would stay in the museums of Canada.

Chapter 4
The Great Canadian Dinosaur Rush

B y 1912, an important American dinosaur hunter by the name of Barnum Brown had been hunting successfully in Alberta for two years. He was named after Phineas T. Barnum, the famous showman of "The Great Traveling World's Fair." Like his namesake, Barnum Brown was a bit of a showman. He was tall and purposeful, with sparkling blue eyes and an impeccable wardrobe. A highly respected bone collector for the American Museum of Natural History, Barnum was rumoured to be able to smell fossils hidden within rock formations.

Barnum came to Alberta in 1910 after meeting an Albertan rancher who had boasted about having a large number of dinosaur bones on his ranch. Wanting to see this apparent goldmine for himself, Barnum was soon exporting a large quantity of bones from the site. With his arrival and successes, Canadians began to notice that a vast number of bones were leaving their country. The federal government had to decide what to do about the bones being exported. Instead of asking non-Canadian dinosaur hunters like Barnum Brown to leave, it was decided that Canada would compete with them. At that time, no Canadian paleontologists were qualified for the job, so, ironically, the federal government hired an American dinosaur hunter to compete with the other American hunters working in Alberta.

Charles Sternberg was 62 years old, but still strong and able, when he agreed to hunt dinosaur bones on Canadian soil in 1912. The Geological Survey of Canada hired Charles to locate fossils in Alberta's badlands and ensure the bones remained in Canada. Charlie and Levi Sternberg were hired to work as his assistants.

George Sternberg, however, had taken a job earlier that year with Barnum Brown. When George had accepted the position, he had no idea he would be

George Sternberg holding the lower jaw of an
Albertosaurus near Steveville, Alberta.

competing against his own family after 17 years of
hunting with them. Charles was eager for his oldest
son to rejoin the Dream Team, but it would be another year before George would complete his contract
with Barnum Brown and return to his father and
brothers.

With two high-profile hunting parties competing for bones in the same area of Alberta, the Great Canadian Dinosaur Rush began.

* * *

Meeting in South Dakota, Charles, Charlie, and Levi prepared for life in the badlands. On a bitterly cold July day, after loading horses and equipment into a freight car, the three men boarded a sleeper car bound for Drumheller. It took them 10 days to make the journey from their homeland to their new lives as employees of the Canadian government.

The train travelled north through the Crow Indian Reserve, where teepee villages stood alongside the railway tracks. Despite the anxiety caused by white settlers moving on to Native land, Charles had not experienced conflict with any Native peoples while hunting for dinosaur bones. But he had come close.

As the train made its way through the rolling countryside, Charles recalled a day late in June of 1876. On that day, a gentle rain had fallen, softening the earth and making conditions perfect for fossil hunting. Charles shouldered his pick and started down a canyon, eagerly scanning the rocks on either side. Soon he came upon a fresh pony trail. Curious about who had made the trail, he decided to follow it.

In a clearing he saw a large band of warriors rest-ing, seeking shelter from the rain beneath antelope skins. They had only recently finished eating, as embers still glowed in the ashes of an extinguished campfire. Horses stood quietly by, tied to the bushes.

Charles silently turned around and left, unno-ticed. It wasn't until later that he learned whom he had seen. The large group of Kiowa, Cheyenne, and Arapaho warriors, led by Crazy Horse, was on its way north to join with Sitting Bull in the fateful battle of Little Big Horn.

Unwilling to give up their land, the Sioux nation was prepared to fight for it. Colonel Custer, with Crow warriors on his side, attacked Sitting Bull's camp. Six weeks later on June 25, 1876, Charles and Edward Cope arrived in Helena, Montana. There they received news that the Sioux had just massacred Colonel Custer about 240 kilometres from the Judith River basin where they were headed.

Charles and Edward Cope were strongly advised against travelling through Montana, where tensions were still running high. Where they were heading was neutral land, a place that neither the Sioux nor the Crow had claimed, but nevertheless it was potentially dangerous territory.

Charles and Cope went anyway. They were

drawn by the possibility of a treasure trove of fossils. Frightened by the warnings, many of their crew abandoned them, but Charles and Cope pressed on. They prospected bones across the river from a Crow village of more than 2000, and became friendly with many people of the Crow nation.

As it turned out, Cope's mouthful of false teeth was of great interest to the Crow peoples. Charles could not be certain, but he believed the teeth were the reason the two bone hunters had been able to work without incident. When it was time for their camp to move, a scout informed them that Sitting Bull's camp was only a day's walk away from their new site. Upon hearing this news, the remaining crew abandoned the expedition. With only a cook left, Charles and Cope continued to hunt for bones. And once again, their hunt was completed without incident.

His reverie over, Charles snapped back to the present. He was looking forward to new adventures on Canadian soil. By evening, the train pulled into Great Falls, Montana. Inspired by the sight of the Missouri River flowing into the falls, Charles began to plan ahead. His team would need a rowboat to travel the rapids of the Red Deer River, and Calgary, he had been told, was the place to acquire one. Conferring with his sons, it was decided that they would travel to Calgary and Charles would stay there until the custom-built boat was complete. In the meantime, the boys would go cross-country with the horse and wagon, and the three would meet again in Drumheller.

Crossing into Alberta at Sweet Grass, Charles bid a silent goodbye to the country that had served him well. For 44 years he had hunted bones in 12 states and located tens of thousands of specimens. During that time, he had witnessed and been a part of many great changes. Wagon trails had been replaced with train tracks carrying great chugging steam engines across the country. White settlers had staked out their homes in the west. Edward Cope and Othniel Marsh, the key players in the bone wars, had died.

Even hunting techniques had changed. When Charles had first hunted fossils with Cope, rice had been a staple of the dinosaur hunting party. The party would take rice and boil it until it thickened. They would then dip cotton cloth, burlap, or flour bags into the rice mixture and use them to bandage the bones. It was a crude process, but not too different from the more current practice of using strips of cloth dipped in plaster of Paris. Charles would use the newer technique to strengthen and transport the bones he planned on finding in Canada.

An Impressive Find

When the Sternbergs arrived in Calgary in 1912, Alberta was still a frontier region. Gradually, the plains Natives had been resettled in reservations, and large portions of the prairies soon belonged to successful cattle ranchers. But ranching was giving way to farming as settlers flooded the West. In the southern part of the province, Mormon Americans were crossing the border to try their hand at farming. It was a frontier region full of optimism and promise.

The Sternbergs were pleased with their new surroundings, and as they made their way along the Red Deer River, not even the swarms of pesky mosquitoes could dampen their enthusiasm. Faces covered with netting, the scent of smudge burning its way into their memories, the Sternberg team reconvened and set up camp near Drumheller.

Camp logistics ran smoothly and food stores were well stocked. Supplies of beans, bacon, and fresh meat were purchased from Drumheller once or twice a month. To keep the food cool and to stop the butter from melting in the heat of the midday sun, the team's cook dug a hole for storage and lined it with burlap.

For the Sternbergs, working six days a week regardless of the weather yielded encouraging results. It didn't take long for the team to locate great numbers of fossilized bones.

Twenty-seven-year-old Charlie made the first major discovery when he found the end of a tibia bone. Realizing that the tip of the bone was merely an indication of something even more wonderful, Charlie quickly got to work uncovering the rest of the bones. What he unearthed just west of Drumheller was the complete skeleton of a duckbilled, bird-hipped dinosaur called *Corythosaurus*.

Excavating this remarkable find proved to be a difficult task, one that would take up most of the remaining season. The skeleton lay on its side, the hind limbs doubled in on themselves, the front ones at right angles to the body. The head was bent towards the front limbs, and the ribcage was intact. The bones were buried in fine, sandy clay, and both clay and bones were cracked in all directions.

Of course, the Sternbergs were professionals; they knew how to lift the thousands of fragmented bone pieces from the earth. The first thing they did was to remove the loose clay and sand, and dig out a floor in the cliff that was large enough for them to work on. They then traced the lateral spines of the

George Sternberg packing dinosaur bones into
a crate near Steveville, Alberta

skeleton with a digger and crooked awl to ensure they did not burrow into the bones themselves. As soon as any bone was exposed, it was instantly treated with shellac varnish and wrapped in rice paper. They dug around the skull, and covered it with burlap soaked in plaster before removing it. Soon the torso was also covered with heavy plaster and burlap that they supported with willow poles. So large was the *Corythosaurus* trunk that it had to be divided in half, each section weighing about the same as two bull elephants. When the excavation was complete, all but the tail had been found.

Eventually, the preparation of each section of the skeleton was finished. The Sternbergs carved stone blocks containing dozens of bones from the cliff, and hoisted them down to the wagon using a tripod. It was precarious work because of the narrow ridge on which they stood.

The earth they had removed from around the skeleton had been used to build a road below so that a wagon could be backed up to the site. Two wooden planks became a runway between the wagon and the bones. Charlie managed the loading of the wagon.

During the loading process, the excavation team edged a particularly large and bulky section of skeleton towards the runway. A group of men below the runway worked to guide the precious block of bones from underneath while another group stood above, lowering the section slowly and putting a great deal of trust in their hoist and tripod. Unfortunately, the block proved to be too large and awkward, and the loaders lost control.

Suddenly the block was hurling towards the wagon at an amazing speed. Men jumped in all directions to avoid the inevitable crash. When the block finally came to a stop, Charlie nervously surveyed the damage. Luckily, this wasn't the first time the Sternbergs had been chased by a dinosaur, so they had been prepared. The careful wrapping that they were known for had prevented any major damage to the bones.

By the end of the season, the Sternbergs had amassed a tremendous quantity of bones to ship to Ottawa. But while it had been a successful summer of bone hunting, the team had struggled with the terrain all summer. They would have to rethink their transportation and equipment needs for when they returned the next spring.

The 1913 Hunting Season
The Sternbergs knew their wagon and boat were inadequate for transporting the mass of fossils they

planned to find during the 1913 season. So, upon arriving in Drumheller that spring, they purchased a five-horsepower motorboat and then built a barge big enough to hold two tents, one for sleeping and one for cooking. Ready to begin another season in the field, the crew began their journey.

Levi took the horses and wagon, and headed south to the town of Steveville, where the team would set up camp. Charlie navigated the waters of the Red Deer River in the motorboat, and Charles followed behind on the barge.

The boat motored slowly along, pulling the barge past scattered islands colonized by cotton-woods. On either side of the river valley were haystack-like mounds of eroded earth, long ridges, and coal seams. But as picturesque as the Red Deer River valley was, the scenery was wasted on Charles. He was impatient with the slow progress they were making down the river. The Sternbergs were eager to begin hunting, knowing that Barnum Brown was also in the area searching for dinosaurs.

As if the weather gods were aware of the need for speed, strong winds blew in from the east. Gradually, the barge began to pick up its pace as the winds filled the tents like sails. Gaining more and more momentum, the barge was soon outpacing the motorboat that was pulling it. Choppy waves crashed over the sides of the barge, washing the floors of the tents with cold river water. For the rest of the trip, Charles was kept busy dismantling the tents and bailing out water.

After 16 hours of adventurous barge sailing, the crew finally made it to camp. They had travelled 128 kilometres downriver to Steveville, situated on the north end of Dead Lodge Canyon.

The Sternbergs set up their camp near Barnum Brown's. The location of both camps was well chosen. A post office and fresh water were very close by, and farmers in the area provided eggs, butter, and chickens to the workers. It would be another summer rich with discoveries.

The two camps enjoyed a friendly rivalry, as there was a wealth of material in the rich fossil beds, plenty for each party. They regularly spent Sundays together, observing the Sabbath in suits and ties. Every week, Charles conducted a service, which was followed by a picnic lunch. When the bull berries were ripe, the men even took time out from fossil hunting to make jam!

Although the competition on Alberta soil was friendly and never reached the level of rivalry that had existed between Edward Cope and Othniel Marsh in the United States, the potential for conflict

Barnum Brown at a dinosaur excavation site in Drumheller, Alberta

was always there. Barnum Brown, known for his short temper, did not like his discoveries to be compromised. Once, while collecting bones on the island of Samos in Greece, he flew into a rage when he was denied an export permit to remove his finds. He proceeded to wage a battle in Athens, using reasoned argument, persuasion by influential friends, and eventually, bribery. He finally received a permit, only to find out that his wife had already smuggled the fossils out on their boat.

George Sternberg finished up his contract with Barnum Brown in the summer of 1913. Somewhat disgruntled that his rivals were so close to his hunting grounds, Brown had grown suspicious of George. He had begun to regard George as a spy, and believed that George was informing his family of Brown's every move. Eager to escape this constant suspicion, George was happy to join forces with his own family again.

With the addition of George, the Sternbergs became the largest party of fossil hunters in the area. They were collectively enthusiastic and keen to outdo each other in their finds.

Charles began to hunt for fossils immediately after disembarking from the barge, even as the water heated up for coffee. He sensed this would be a rich area to hunt.

Charlie was first to prove his father right. Not long after their arrival, he found the remains of a huge carnivore near their camp. The ribs, head, and hind limbs of the skeleton lay visible high on a steep slope.

When they died, dinosaurs did not take into consideration the dinosaur hunters who would one day be tasked with tracking them down. Frequently the dinosaurs took their last breath in the most inconvenient of places. This was one of those dinosaurs.

Digging out a narrow bench in the cliff to work from, Charlie began to excavate. It was another extremely large skeleton, and its excavation and transportation was as difficult as that of the skeleton that had crashed down the hill the previous summer.

Charlie decided to remove his new find in two sections. The entire length of the skeleton, from teeth to tail, was 8.7 metres. The skull alone was 91 cm long and about the size of a child's bicycle. All the teeth were in place, double-edged and serrated. The hind legs had three clawed toes, and the front legs had two. When it lived, the dinosaur must have looked ferocious as it skulked across the marshy plains in search of prey, its teeth glistening.

The only thing standing between the prepared skeleton and Ottawa, where the bones were to be sent, was the terribly steep cliff on which the bones lay. In order to transport the skeleton, a narrow ridge, not much wider than the wagon, had to be dug out of the canyon side. A glance below to the boulder-filled gorge confirmed that there was no margin for error. When the time came to load the bones, the wagon was carefully backed to the excavation site. The bones, precious and incredibly heavy, had to be safeguarded. One horse's misstep, or a slippery section for a wagon wheel, and the whole load — men and all — would careen over the edge of the cliff and be shattered to pieces in the gorge below.

Charlie oversaw the entire nerve-wracking transportation process. He had complete faith in the men and horses, but still he held his breath as he watched the slow-moving wagon creep forwards along the ridge. Occasionally he would exhale, give the team a direction, then hold his breath and watch again. His trust was rewarded. Nothing was lost down the side of the deep gorge.

Six weeks of strenuous work to excavate, wrap, and transport the bones had been worth it. The skeleton was identified as an *Albertosaurus libratus,* and it was the most perfect skeleton of an *Albertosaurus* known to science at the time.

While Charlie had been working on his own find, Charles, George, and Levi had excavated a *Corythosaurus* and a *Chasmosaurus.* The *Chasmosaurus* was an armoured dinosaur with a nose horn and frill spikes.

As the two skeletons were being excavated and prepared for transport, Charles made another important discovery. After a rainshower, he had gone for a walk along a boulder-filled coulee not far from

Steveville and the Happy Jack Ferry. As he attempted to scale a steep slope, he caught sight of two horns poking out from the damp earth. On closer inspection, he realized he had found a skull. The nasal passages and much of the face of the skull had disintegrated from exposure to rain and frost, but the complete lower jaw had survived. As it turned out, Charles had found a *Styracosaurus,* a heavily armoured plant eater known to have had the largest skull of any of the dinosaurs.

Later that summer, Levi found the tail of a crested duckbill dinosaur exposed in a mass of clay on a precipice along a trail. Charlie then found two more specimens in the same quarry, and then another! Four skeletons waited to be unearthed, and four happy paleontologists were eager to unearth them.

It was hard not to get overexcited or greedy when so many amazing specimens were found. But Charles knew the perils of haste, and had taught his sons to excavate with extreme patience and complete control. Each step along the way was painstaking. From the initial blasting of tons of rock, to the intricate removal of each piece of bone; from the cleaning and scraping of each section, to the plastering process, every stage of an excavation was crucial.

The men worked steadily on their finds. The

days were getting shorter, the sun less intense, and the mosquitoes less irritating. Summer was ending. The Sternberg team had already collected a number of dinosaurs, including a *ceratops* (a horned, plant-eating quadruped), a *trachodontidae* (a duckbilled, plant-eating dinosaur), and several theropods (flesh-eating dinosaurs). The quarry of four dinosaur skeletons rounded out the summer's discoveries. However, there was no time to remove the last of the finds, so the Sternberg party covered the last four skeletons with plenty of earth and marked the spot so they could return there the following summer.

Chapter 5
War and Change

I n the summer of 1914, as World War I was beginning in Europe, the dinosaur hunters were back at work in Alberta's badlands. Caught up in the excitement of making new discoveries, these men felt far removed from the events that were taking place overseas.

The Sternberg family returned to the Red Deer River Valley in July of 1914 and made a new camp in Dead Lodge Canyon. In the intense heat of the summer, they rapidly uncovered new skeletons, and this time, George was leading the way.

Among George's first finds was the skeleton of a

Chasmosaurus belli, a horned dinosaur named for the great chasms cut into its crest and skull. George quickly followed that find up with the discovery of the skull of a duckbill called *Centrosaurus monoclonius,* and the partial skeleton of an armoured dinosaur called *Euoplocephalus.*

Though the Sternbergs seemed to have a great deal of success on their hunts, not all of their digs went smoothly, and not all of them led to complete skeletons. In fact, some digs were utter disappointments. Once, after having spotted a tail sticking out from the clay, the team removed tons of rock from the site only to discover that the rest of the skeleton was not there. On another occasion, Charlie Sternberg figured a skeleton was laying in one direction only to find, after days of arduous excavation, that it in fact lay in the opposite direction.

Cold winds and violent storms made digging hazardous, and often delayed fossil hunting for days. Windy afternoons would find any one of the Sternbergs clinging to a steep and barren slope and waiting with bated breath for the gusts to die down.

When it wasn't rainy or windy, it was hot, dry, and dusty. Often the men worked up such a thirst during a long day of excavation that they would spend much of the evening face down in the river drinking water until they could drink no more. Then, with feet too swollen to walk, they would crawl on their hands and knees to bed.

Despite the inherent hunting hazards, the four years they spent together on Canadian soil were successful and happy ones for the Sternberg Dream Team. Together they found, excavated, and shipped to Ottawa 16 whole or partial skeletons of duckbills, hadrosaurs, anklyosaurs, a *Styracosaurus,* and other armoured dinosaurs. But by the end of the 1915 season, the men had become restless, and the ramifications of World War I had started to affect their world.

After Canada joined the war in the summer of 1914, the economy was booming, but there was a shortage of many important minerals and fuels. Although there was a shift in the Geological Survey's funding to support the war efforts, at first there was still a little money left to maintain the Sternberg's work in the West.

However, as time passed and the war continued in Europe, funding for dinosaur hunting grew scarce. When the news reached Charles Sternberg that there was no longer any Canadian federal funding to support his lifework, he resigned from the Geological Survey of Canada, as did his son Levi. George and Charlie continued on as employees, but prospected on a smaller scale.

Barnum Brown also ended his six-year dig in the badlands of Alberta, returning to the American Museum of Natural History with a railway car loaded with fossils. The Canadian Dinosaur Rush was coming to an end.

Charles and Levi soon found work with the British Museum in London, England. Although Britain was in the midst of the war, there were still resources to hire two of the members of the Sternberg team. They returned to the field southeast of Steveville backed this time by British money.

True to their reputation, Charles and Levi found three excellent duckbill skeletons and secured a total of 45 large boxes of bones that summer. One of their duckbill skeletons was almost complete, and even had some of its skin impressions preserved. The excavation of this particular find was quite difficult. Measuring almost nine metres, the skeleton was buried in a treacherous slope inaccessible by horse and wagon. Levi worked long days cutting steps into the steep slope, and then laboriously carried in the water, plaster, and supplies that were needed for excavation.

To remove the prepared bones, father and son built a sled road that stretched for 9.6 kilometres, and the heavy bones were dragged along the road to the prairie, where they were be properly loaded and shipped overseas to London

On a cold and snowy September day in 1916, two of the fossil skeletons were loaded onto the ship S.S. *Mount Temple* leaving Canada for England. Bombs continued to fall in Europe. Though the dinosaur bones had survived for tens of millions of years, they did not survive the perilous journey through the war-torn waters of the Atlantic Ocean. The S.S. *Mount Temple* was torpedoed and sunk by a German submarine, and the bottom of the Atlantic Ocean became the final resting place for the Alberta dinosaur bones. Charles was devastated. The thought of the precious fossils in their watery grave and the wasted time and effort was almost too much for him to bear.

By now, British Museum funds were tight. Charles and Levi spent one more season in the badlands, during which time they found a medium-sized *Albertosaurus,* a complete skeleton of a *Corythosaurus,* and a skull and partial skeleton of a small armoured *Panoplosaurus.*

Charles tried to sell all three finds to the British Museum to replace the skeletons that had been lost at sea. Unfortunately, the museum no longer had money to pay for the skeletons. That did it. It was time for 65-year-old Charles Sternberg to retire. The Sternberg dynasty had come to an end, and each of the men began to follow independent dreams.

Charles Sternberg

Charles left Canada for Kansas in 1917, but his life as a dinosaur hunter was not quite over. Before his death in 1943 at the age of 93, he crossed America many times in search of more bones.

Charles H. Sternberg was the last of the old-time dinosaur hunters. When he began hunting fossils, he relied upon horses and wagons. By the time he retired, plane travel was a possibility. His work ushered in the new age of modern paleontology. More importantly, his passion for this work helped to spark interest in dinosaurs not only within his own family, but among other amateur and professional hunters as well.

Charles played a significant role in the development of Canadian paleontology. Over the course of his career he collected magnificent fossils, most of which stayed in Canada. Tens of thousands of specimens, including many original discoveries, were a result of his lifetime commitment to dinosaur hunting.

George F. Sternberg

George continued to work for the Geological Survey until 1915, at which time the work dried up and he returned to Kansas. Five years later, he was hired by the University of Alberta to collect bones and prepare them for display. By 1921 George was back in the badlands of Alberta, hunting for dinosaurs.

While wandering the badlands, George noticed three small, perfectly preserved teeth glistening in the sun. Within an hour he had the area surrounding the teeth laid bare, and there before him lay a remarkable skull and most of a skeleton. Noticing that the dome-like skull was enormously thick, George suspected he had unearthed something unusual and important.

Taking the skull with him, he returned to camp and began to do some research. He wrote a letter to the University of Alberta describing his find. When a letter was returned to him, George had a name for his latest discovery. It was the skeleton of a *Troodon,* a lightly built meat-eater that had large, slashing claws and pointy, saw-edged teeth.

After his time in Alberta, George Sternberg went on to work for the Field Museum of Natural History in Chicago, and then in Patagonia in southern Argentina. Eventually he gave up freelance dinosaur hunting for museum work at the Fort Hays Kansas Teachers College. He died at the age of 86, a world-renowned fossil hunter with only a fifth-grade education.

Charlie Sternberg

Charlie's interests had always gone beyond merely hunting for dinosaur bones. When his father left the Canadian business of dinosaur hunting and the Sternberg team disbanded, Charlie left Alberta. He moved back to Kansas and began to study and write about the fossils that he had dedicated his life to uncovering, cleaning, and assembling.

Not totally ready to abandon the life his father had introduced him to, Charlie continued to hunt for fossils in the Wood Mountain Settlement in Saskatchewan, the same area in which George Dawson had found the first of the Canadian dinosaurs 47 years earlier. Charlie led 13 expeditions to the area and added to the collection of the Geological Survey of Canada and the National Museum of Ottawa. He was also responsible for mapping the fossil sites, and was a consultant on the creation of the Provincial Dinosaur Park in Alberta.

The construction of the Calgary Zoo began in 1927. Charlie Sternberg was a consultant on the production of a series of 50 dinosaur models and other prehistoric animals constructed out of cement. The last model to be built was a dramatic *Brontosaurus* with a heavy body and legs, and a long neck and tail. The model was named "Dinny." Today, Dinny is known to be an *Apatosaurus* and has become the zoo's mascot. Standing 11 metres tall and weighing in at 120 tonnes, Dinny continues to welcome visitors to the Calgary Zoo.

Charlie continued to work in the dinosaur business right up to his death in 1981. He passed away just a few days before his 96th birthday.

Levi Sternberg

When the Sternberg team separated, Levi remained in the Red Deer River area as a freelance dinosaur hunter working mainly for the British Museum of Natural History. The University of Toronto then employed him as head collector and preparator and he found himself back in the Red Deer River valley, where he had first gone with his brothers and his father 22 years earlier.

Time had changed the valley. The forces of erosion had exposed new rock strata. New bones still surfaced even after many years of dinosaur hunting in the area. Levi worked feverishly to uncover the new specimens.

As he was excavating the bones of a *Styracosaurus,* he realized that the lower jawbone he uncovered was one his family had searched for 22 years earlier. It took a few years, but this jawbone was eventually reunited with the rest of the skeleton he and his family had discovered more than two decades earlier.

Levi, like the rest of the men in his family, was a meticulous collector and a hard worker. He eventually retired in 1962, and died 15 years later at the age of 82.

Chapter 6
A Modern Dinosaur Hunter: Philip Currie

The years surrounding World War I were important ones for paleontology in Canada, but while the scientific community was pleased with its various dinosaur discoveries, the public took little interest.

When the Great Depression of the 1930s hit, dinosaur hunting slowed considerably. The Canadian government was more concerned with stabilizing the economy than with hunting for prehistoric bones. Official work was held back even more during World War II.

To boost public interest, various Canadian

museums began to display dinosaur bones and publish articles and books on paleontology. By the 1950s, curiosity in dinosaurs was on the rise. Movies, books, and articles in popular magazines breathed new life into the ancient creatures.

During this period, the lives of the dinosaur hunters also changed, most noticeably in terms of their equipment and techniques. Computers, scanners, x-ray machines, and satellites were all used to search and understand the fossil links to the past.

Theories about the dinosaurs were changing as well. Until the beginning of the 19th century, some people believed the calculations of Irish Archbishop James Ussher, who determined that the date and time of the creation of Earth was October 23, 4004 B.C. at 9 A.M., making it roughly 6000 years old. By the 20th century, the general consensus among dinosaur hunters like Barnum Brown and Charles Sternberg was that the Cretaceous period was less than three million years ago. Today, scientists have established that the "Age of the Dinosaurs" peaked between 80 and 65 million years ago.

As the 20th century progressed, hunting and camp locations for paleontologists began to change, too. Steveville, Alberta, once the hotspot for dinosaur hunters who relied on it for supplies, mail, baths, and entertainment, became a ghost town in 1962.

And as hunting techniques and locations were changing, so were the identities of the hunters themselves. By the latter half of the 20th century, most of Canada's early dinosaur hunters had either retired or passed away, and new ones were arriving on the scene. Among these contemporary hunters was Dr. Philip Currie, who is now curator of dinosaurs at the Royal Tyrrell Museum in Drumheller. Philip Currie's career began in 1976, when he moved to Alberta following his doctoral studies at McGill University to take a job as a field paleontologist for the Provincial Museum of Alberta, in Edmonton.

Since his move to Alberta, Philip has worked tirelessly to uncover the mysteries of the dinosaurs. Like his predecessors, he is exhilarated by each new discovery that is made in the field of paleontology. His breath is still taken away by the questions that arise when each new fossil is contemplated. How many kinds of dinosaurs were there? How did they live? How did they evolve? How did they act? What did they look like? These are questions that Dr. Philip Currie has been asking for years.

More recently, Philip has contemplated the mysteries of how dinosaurs socialized. Were they solitary animals? How did they reproduce and care for their young? He has found some of the answers in the fossilized egg nests and embryos of southern Alberta.

Most Exciting Eggs

Philip Currie admits to being determined and driven, and believes those two words are nicer ways of saying that he is stubborn. He has been hunting dinosaur bones, as well as eggs *and* embryos, for over 25 years. His research station is in Alberta's badlands, where he enjoys the perfect combination of fieldwork, research at the Royal Tyrrell Museum, and a little healthy competition from friends and fellow researchers.

Dr. Jack Horner is a fellow paleontologist and curator at the Museum of the Rockies in Bozema, Montana. He hunts for dinosaurs in the United States, and in the 1990s served as technical adviser for the movies *Jurassic Park* and *The Lost World.* Over the years, Dr. Horner has provided just the kind of healthy competition that keeps dinosaur hunting interesting for Dr. Currie.

It had long been established that Alberta was once home to the huge Cretaceous dinosaurs *Albertosaurus* and *Tyrannosaurus rex,* smaller theropods *Troodon* and *Dromaeosaurus,* and their numerous prey, hadrosaurs and ceratopsians. After finding several of these dinosaur skeletons in the province, Philip Currie wanted to track down other evidence in the fossil record — dinosaur eggs.

Jack Horner had been uncovering dinosaur eggs in Montana since 1979 in an area where dinosaur bones were not plentiful. Knowing of Philip's desire to find eggs north of the border, Jack often joked with him that there were no eggs to be found in Alberta. Philip, in return, joked that there were no skeletons to be found in Montana. Despite their good-natured ribbing, each scientist desperately wanted to locate for himself what was plentiful in the other's field area.

Each kept searching. Jack continued to find dinosaur eggs, some of which even contained embryos — dinosaur babies that had not yet hatched when they were killed. Ribbing his Canadian counterpart, he challenged Philip to "get off his butt" and find at least one egg. Not one to back down from a challenge, Philip vowed to do just that. But then Jack took a strong lead in their race.

Jack moved his dig site to a high, dry, and sandy area in northern Montana, just a stone's throw away from the Alberta border. It was there that he finally found a skeleton. Much to his delight, it proved to be the skeleton of a baby dinosaur. Soon after this discovery, Jack found another skeleton, as well as several eggs and embryos. It seemed he was hitting the jackpot as an edgy Philip continued to search for eggs.

Not long after Jack's skeleton discoveries, the Alberta government announced plans to build a reservoir along the Milk River. Philip flew south by helicopter to the land along the western edge of the Milk River system. He went on a preliminary survey to see what potential remains might be lost in the event the a dam was built and the area submerged.

This land, 160 kilometres south of Dinosaur Provincial Park, and close to the Montana border and Jack Horner's camp, was the perfect spot for finding dinosaur bones.

When the helicopter landed on the Milk River ridge, Philip was anxious to disembark and begin exploring. Breathing in the dry air, he scanned the dusty rocks, eyed the milky white river, then took a purposeful step down from the helicopter. But just as he made contact with the hot earth below, he lost his footing and both legs suddenly shot out from under him.

Philip Currie, head curator of the Royal Tyrrell Museum and one of the leading vertebrate researchers in the world, had fallen over! Startled, he scrambled to his feet, and suddenly realized that he was back in the game with Jack Horner.

As it turned out, Philip had fallen on a kind of

rock called *caliche,* an immature form of hardpan. Caliche occurs when soil in dry areas turns to rock and is fused together. In its early stages, caliche begins as nodules forming in the soil. The nodules, in this case, acted like ball bearings.

Dinosaur eggs had been hard to find in Alberta because the province's sediments are typically too acidic. These acidic conditions worked to dissolve the shells of any eggs before they could turn into stone. But Philip knew that a presence of caliche indicated that there had been an abundance of salt deposited into the soil in that area around 75 million years ago. This salt would have produced the right pH balance for preserving eggs. Brushing the dust from his pants, Philip was back on his feet and eager to begin exploring.

The helicopter pilot, knowing he was in the company of one of the world's leading paleontologists, asked to see some bones. Obligingly, Philip took a few steps and picked up a small bone fragment. Not easily impressed, the pilot wanted to see something more complete. Philip turned his trained eye back to the earth. Right beside his boot was a whole bone from a baby dinosaur. Even if the pilot was not satisfied with this find, Philip was. Baby dinosaurs were rare in Alberta. He had a good feeling about the area along the Milk River.

Despite the area's perfect conditions and Philip's eagerness to prove that his hunch was correct, it was too late to hunt extensively. The 1996 summer season had already been planned. Philip and his crew were committed to other digs in Alberta and China. However, they made plans to free up three weeks in the following season to take a more intensive look at the area. They hoped three weeks would prove enough time to find eggs in Alberta's sandstone.

When the 1997 hunting season arrived, Philip made some final preparations for his trip back to the Milk River and tied up loose ends on other projects. Then, three days before he was due to leave, he received a phone call that interrupted all his plans. The call was from Dr. Len Hills, a professor at the University of Calgary. Hills claimed that his 19-year-old student assistant, Wendy Sloboda, had found fragments of dinosaur eggs near Warner, Alberta, which was located just north of the Milk River.

Amazed at the propitious timing of this piece of news, Philip Currie drove to Calgary to meet Dr. Hills and take a look at the specimens. When he opened the specimen box, Philip saw black, slightly curved fossil fragments, all of which were covered with a tight pattern of tiny pinpricks. There was no doubt in

Philip's mind about what the young Wendy Sloboda had found: they were quite clearly dinosaur shell fragments.

A couple of days later, Philip Currie and two technicians, Kevin Aulenback and Gerhard Maier, drove south to the Milk River Ridge. After checking into a small hotel, Wendy Sloboda took the eager scientists to where she had found the egg fragments. The site was located along the north side of the Milk River Ridge, not far from where Philip had fallen the previous year. The team prospected the area immediately, and sure enough, Wendy's site revealed thousands of eggshell fragments. It was a dinosaur nest. Unfortunately, the huge nest had been badly eroded, and all that remained were lots of small triangular shell pieces.

Eager to find better preserved egg fossils, the team decided to push on. They explored the area as far west as Waterton Park. Nearing the end of the three week hunt, they had found evidence of 12 eggshell sites, but no eggs.

Determination outweighed disappointment, and the team wasn't planning to give up just yet. Philip took the group across the border to Jack Horner's camp in Montana. There, the Canadian dinosaur hunters had a close look at the eggs the

Americans had found, and at the rocky hillside in which the eggs had been discovered. The Canadians returned to Alberta knowing exactly what fossilized dinosaur eggs looked like and what environmental conditions were necessary for their preservation. They were ready to hunt again.

Waking long before the sun was up, Philip, Kevin, and Gerhard began another day of egg hunting. The egg site in Montana had reminded Wendy of a section of the Milk River Ridge where she had played as a child. It was an area of fantastically eroded hoodoos and soaring, gentle bluffs. She took the team there, and they began their day looking at some flood plain deposits on a local farmer's land. Philip felt the conditions were ideal. He was right. Nestled in the rock layers was the first nest of well-preserved eggs found in Alberta.

Dinosaur eggs are not the same shape as chicken eggs. Some are long and oblong shaped like baguettes of bread, while others are the size and shape of volleyballs. The curved surface of a fossil egg is crushed, warped and usually black. The bottoms of the eggs are generally well preserved, while the tops have been eroded by the elements. Often, the insides of the eggs have been scoured by the same processes of erosion and are filled with sediment.

Satisfied with the egg find, but still having a little more time to hunt, the team kept on looking. Farther down-canyon along the ridge, they made their next discovery.

This time it was Gerhard Maier who found a scree of eggshell fragments and a bone. It was the upper leg bone of a duckbill dinosaur, and it was very small. Most adult dinosaur leg bones are roughly 1.2 metres in length, about as tall as a 10-year-old child, but this bone was less than 7 or 8 centimetres long, about the length of a pencil.

Philip Currie was very excited. Not only had they found their first nest of preserved eggs, but now they could add the discovery of the bones of a baby duckbill to their list of accomplishments. Buoyed by the day's discoveries, the team extended their expedition one more day to see if they could find scientific proof that the leg bone had come from an egg, making it a bone of an embryo and not the bone of a baby.

The small group of paleontologists approached the farmer whose land they had been exploring earlier that morning for permission to go back on his property one more time. Reluctantly, the farmer gave his permission, and the team wasted no time collecting numerous small bones from the egg nest. Kevin Aulenback, tired with bone picking, left the others to walk along the scree one more time.

Philip had only hours left before commitments in Dinosaur Provincial Park, the Royal Tyrrell Museum, and China would pull the team away from the Milk River Ridge. The men did not waste any time; it was their last day.

By noon, the hour of departure, no new discoveries had been made and preparations for leaving began. Kevin Aulenback, usually a punctual man, had not returned to the group. The other men waited, scanning the hills for a sign of their missing team member. After half an hour went by, Kevin came running over the hill like a runaway train. Philip could not make out a single word he was shouting as he approached. A fast talker by nature, Kevin was talking even more quickly than usual. His colleagues had never seen him so wound up. They listened hard, for they knew he had something important to say.

Finally, the words, "Babies in eggs! Babies in eggs!" were audible in his excited chatter. The team had already found babies *and* eggs, but babies *in* eggs was an entirely different matter. It was what they had been searching for! Those three magic words prompted the world-class team to scramble over the hills like a pack of hungry wolves in pursuit of their next meal. Full of anticipation, they made their way

Philip Currie in the field

down to the coulee where Kevin had been hunting.

Instantly, all three men were on their hands and knees examining the hardpan and sifting through the loose eggshell fragments. Sure enough, they came across tiny hadrosaur bones inside a circle of eggshell. The bones were so small that the team was able to quickly deduce they were not the bones of baby dinosaurs, but of embryos.

Laughing with joy, the men picked up bone after bone. They were beside themselves with the richness of their find. With all thoughts of departure now pushed aside, they continued to explore the area. Gerhard Maier found an egg with an articulated tail in it, and Philip picked up a tiny jawbone with a set of perfect tiny teeth. Pretty soon all three men were dancing around, shaking hands, and saying, "Pinch me! No, don't pinch me!"

There was no doubt in their minds that this bed of eggs, embryos, and bones was an incredibly valuable find. However, the men weren't quite sure what to do with their ancient treasure trove. Knowing that their high level of excitement was impairing their ability to act logically and carefully, they decided it was best to leave the site, return to their regular duties, and confer with other scientists and technicians over what to do next.

Their collection bags filled, the team left the coulee and sought out the farmer to share their exciting news with him. The farmer, however, was not thrilled. After all, the find was on his farm, and the farm was his home. His family enjoyed picnics and took regular walks in the area that the men had been exploring. Dinosaur bones and eggs meant unwanted attention and disruption to his life. Annoyed, he told the dumbfounded egg hunters that he might not let them back on his land. This warning concerned the scientists, and they returned home with mixed emotions.

Headline News
Upon his return from the Milk River expedition, Philip Currie enjoyed a peaceful weekend. He spent much of Saturday and Sunday unpacking leisurely and preparing for his next hunt in China's Gobi Desert. Then, at 10 o'clock on Sunday evening, the phone rang and everything changed. The caller was a reporter with *Calgary Herald* who had just one question for Philip: had he really found dinosaur eggs and embryos? The story was ready to go to print, the newspaper just needed confirmation that the scoop was true. A very flabbergasted Philip hung up on the reporter and called the museum.

Knowing there was no way to suppress this news, Philip called the reporter back, clarified some of the article's details, and waited for his copy of the morning paper. It was a complete mystery how the story had left his team and reached the office of the *Calgary Herald.*

Philip didn't get much sleep that night. At 4 A.M. *The New York Times* called. The story had gone international. After that, the phone continued to ring for the rest of the day and for many days following.

When the news was first leaked, Philip was receiving a phone call every three minutes. This was the most intensive interest he had ever experienced over one of his finds. In fact, it was pandemonium for the paleontologist.

The source of the leak was traced back to a dig site where Kevin and Gerhard had gone immediately after the Milk River trip. In the summer months, digs are often home to university students and volunteers eager to learn more about paleontology. One of the volunteers on this particular dig was a reporter from the *Calgary Herald.* Upon hearing the story from an excited technician, the volunteer made a phone call to the newspaper office in Calgary, and the story was out.

Sensitive to the farmer's fear of loss of privacy, the exact location of the discovery was not revealed to anyone. But the secrecy surrounding the find just served to increase public interest. The site was an extremely valuable fossil resource, and journalists, amateur fossil hunters, and members of the general public wanted desperately to know where it was.

Reporters flooded the Milk River area, interviewing residents and attempting to piece together the route of the dinosaur hunters. Planes flew overhead trying to locate the excavation site. One person even went so far as to pose as an agricultural inspector to gain access to farms where the site was thought to be.

* * *

The government of Alberta began negotiations with the farmer for his land. The farm needed to be purchased or traded so that the site could be explored freely. After several months of intense negotiations, a deal was sealed. The paleontologists and technicians obtained access to their 75 million-year-old nursery once again. Upon their return to the site, the team was thrilled to see that their find was even better than they remembered.

As he worked on the Milk River site, Philip Currie found dozens of dinosaur nests, plus remains of dinosaurs ranging in age from embryonic to adult.

The discovery of this multi-generational grave questioned the theory that dinosaurs were solitary creatures. Not only was Philip's site rich with eggs, but it held evidence of a group of dinosaurs that died en masse. Did large herbivores travel in herds? Did vicious predators hunt in packs? Did mother dinosaurs care for their young long after they had hatched? The answers to these questions were getting closer to being answered.

The bones of the dinosaurs found ranged in size. Some were the tiny bones of embryos; others were 10 times larger. The evidence presented by this range of bone size indicated that young dinosaurs lived in groups with animals of all sizes. The discovery of eggs, embryos, and skeletal bones suggested that mother dinosaurs cared for their young. Finding so many bones together suggested that dinosaurs lived and died in herds.

Philip's successful hunt for dinosaur eggs ended with a bonus. After pooling his finds with Jack Horner's specimens in Montana, he realized his Canadian eggs and embryos were different than the eggs and embryos that Jack was finding. Philip's finds were evidence of a new species, *Hypacrosaurus stebingeri*, which was a large, bipedal high-crested hadrosaur measuring about eight metres long. No

Hypacrosaurus remains had been found in Montana or in Dinosaur Provincial Park, two areas close to the Milk River. This seemed to confirm the theory that a great diversity of dinosaurs existed in Cretaceous times.

The farmland, rich with dinosaur fossils, became known as Devil's Coulee, an historic site and field area for the Royal Tyrrell Museum in southern Alberta.

The friendly competition between Philip Currie and Jack Horner regarding egg discoveries ended in a draw. Both scientists now had eggs, embryos, and juvenile skeletons to study. But there is sure to be new competition sparked as each paleontologist searches for clues to support his ever-evolving understanding of the period 80 to 65 million years ago when dinosaurs ruled the earth.

Epilogue

For the last 200 years, a select group of men and women have dedicated their lives to hunting for dinosaurs in Canada. Driven by a desire to understand the mysteries of the "terrible lizard," these scientists have embarked on incredible adventures, enduring endless frustrations and reaping astonishing rewards.

Through the remarkable efforts of these men and women, more than 50 genera of dinosaur have been unearthed on Canadian soil. And while these finds have helped us to make some sense of our prehistoric past, the answers to many more ancient mysteries still lay hidden in the badlands of Alberta and other parts of Canada, waiting to be uncovered by a new generation of dinosaur hunters.

Bibliography

Barkhouse, Joyce C. *George Dawson, the Little Giant.* Vancouver: Clarke, Irwin & Company, 1974.

Chalmers, William. *George Mercer Dawson. Geologist, Scientist, Explorer.* Montreal: XYZ Publishing, 2000.

Grady, Wayne. *The Dinosaur Project: The Story of the Greatest Dinosaur Expedition Ever Mounted.* Toronto: Macfarlane Walter & Ross, 1993.

Inglis, Alex. *Northern Vagabond: The Life and Career of J.B. Tyrell.* Toronto: McClelland & Stewart, 1978.

Rogers, Katherine. *The Sternberg Fossil Hunters: A Dinosaur Dynasty.* Missoula: Mountain Press Publishing Company, 1991.

Spalding, David. *Into the Dinosaurs' Graveyard Canadian Digs and Discoveries.* Toronto: Doubleday Canada, 1999.

Bibliography

Sternberg, Charles, H. *Hunting Dinosaurs in the Bad Lands of the Red Deer River, Alberta, Canada.* Edmonton: First NeWest Press Edition, 1985.

Appendix 1
Dinosaur Data

Name	Meaning of name	Length	How it walked	Type of feeder	When it lived	Dinosaur group
Albertosaurus	Alberta lizard	9 m	on 2 legs	Canirvore	76-74 mya	theropod
Apatosaurus	Deceptive lizard	23 m	on 4 legs	Herbivore	154-145 mya	sauropod
Centrasaurus	Well-horned lizard	6.1 m	on 4 legs	Herbivore	76-74 mya	ceratopian
Chasmosaurus	Ravince lizard	5.2 m	on 4 legs	Herbivore	80-65 mya	ceratopian
Corythosaurus	Helmet lizard	8-9 m	on 2 legs	Herbivore	76-74 mya	hadrosaur
Dromaeosaurus	Running lizard	1.8 m	on 2 legs	Carnivore	76-74 mya	theropod
Edmontosaurus	Edmonton lizard	13 m	2 or 4 legs	Herbivore	71-65 mya	ornithopod
Euoplocephalus	Well-protected head	12 m	on 4 legs	Herbivore	71 mya	anklyosaur
Hypocrosaurus	High-ridged lizard	7.5-9 m	2 or 4 legs	Herbivore	72-70 mya	hadrosaur
Panoplosaurus	Armoured lizard	4.5 m	on 4 legs	Herbivore	76-73 mya	anklyosaur
Triceratops	Three-horned face	9 m	on 4 legs	Herbivore	72-67 mya	ceratopian
Troodon	Wounding tooth	2 m	on 2 legs	Carnivore	76-74 mya	theropod
Tyrannosaurus	Tyrant lizard	12 m	on 2 legs	Carnivore	67-65 mya	theropod
Styracosaurus	Spiked lizard	5.5 m	on 4 legs	Herbivore	85-80 mya	ceratopian

mya = million years ago

Acknowledgments

I would like to thank the following individuals who helped me with my research, writing and editing, and by entertaining Maxwell and Charlie so I could write: Philip Currie, Eva Koppelhus, James Lamb, Alice Lamb, Tom Murphy, Marg Murphy, Kara Turner, Joan Dixon, Cathy Beveridge, Frances Hern, Sherile Reilly, Sherring Amsden, Tiffany Mak, Robert Holmes, Colleen Anderson, and friends on 11a Street and 12th Street.

I would also like to acknowledge certain books that were particularly helpful in the course of my research. Dr. Michael Benton's *Dinosaur and Other Prehistoric Animal Factfinder*, Dorling Kindersley Readers' *Dinosaur Detectives*, Dougal Dixon's *Dinosaurs Fossil Hunters*, Edith Fowke's *Folklore of Canada*, Jack Hodgins' *A Passion for Narrative*, Monique Keiran's *Albertosaurus: Death of a Predator*, and Louie Psihoyos and John Knoebber's *Hunting Dinosaurs*.

About the Author

Lisa Murphy-Lamb was born in Kamloops, B.C. and grew up in Calgary. Throughout an educational career that included a B.Ed. from the University of Calgary and an M.Ed with a specialty in inclusive education from McGill, Lisa has focussed on ways to enlighten and educate learners of all ages and abilities. From this basis and philosophy, telling stories, and ultimately writing, were natural extensions. A lifelong and avid traveller, Lisa's journeys across the globe have given her a rich palate from which to draw her narrative.

Lisa lives in Calgary with her husband, James, and two full-time dinosaur hunters, Maxwell (six) and Charlie (three). Their roars can be heard for miles.

Photograph Credits
Cover photograph: Barry Jennings, ViewCalgary; Barry Jennings, ViewCalgary: page 46; Douglas Leighton: page 106; Glenbow Archives: page 17 (NA-249-1), page 66 (NA-3250-13), page 73 (NA-3250-10), page 78 (NA-3596-138); The Thomas Fisher Rare Book Library, University of Toronto: page 30.

OTHER AMAZING STORIES

ISBN	Title	Author
1-55153-983-7	Alberta Titans	Susan Warrender
1-55153-996-9	Emily Carr	Cat Klerks
1-55153-992-6	Ghost Town Stories from the Red Coat Trail	Johnnie Bachusky
1-55153-993-4	Ghost Town Stories from the Canadian Rockies	Johnnie Bachusky
1-55153-994-2	The Heart of a Horse	Gayle Bunney
1-55153-979-9	Ma Murray	Stan Sauerwein
1-55153-986-1	Tales from the West Coast	Adrienne Mason
1-55153-999-3	Mary Schäffer	Jill Foran
1-55153-962-4	Niagara Daredevils	Cheryl MacDonald
1-55153-981-0	Rattenbury	Stan Sauerwein
1-55153-991-8	Rebel Women	Linda Kupecek
1-55153-995-0	Rescue Dogs	Dale Portman
1-55153-998-5	Romance in the Rockies	Kim Mayberry
1-55153-997-7	Sam Steele	Holly Quan
1-55153-985-3	Tales from the Backcountry	Dale Portman
1-55153-989-6	Vancouver's Old-Time Scoundrels	Jill Foran
1-55153-977-2	War Heroes of the RCAF	Cynthia Faryon
1-55153-987-X	Wilderness Tales	Peter Christensen
1-55153-990-X	West Coast Adventures	Adrienne Mason
1-55153-980-2	Women Explorers	Helen Rolfe

These titles are available wherever you buy books. If you have trouble finding the book you want, call the Altitude order desk at 1-800-957-6888, e-mail your request to: orderdesk@altitudepublishing.com or visit our Web site at www.amazingstories.ca

All titles retail for $9.95 Cdn or $7.95 US. (Prices subject to change.)

New AMAZING STORIES titles are published every month. If you would like more information, e-mail your name and mailing address to: amazingstories@altitudepublishing.com.